THE Best OF Buttermilk, BASIN

A Bevy of Cotton and Wool Quilted Projects

Stacy West

The Best of Buttermilk Basin:
A Bevy of Cotton and Wool Quilted Projects
© 2018 by Stacy West

Martingale®
19021 120th Ave. NE, Ste. 102
Bothell, WA 98011-9511 USA
ShopMartingale.com

Printed in China
23 22 21 20 19 18   8 7 6 5 4 3 2 1

Library of Congress Cataloging-in-Publication Data
is available upon request.

ISBN: 978-1-60468-953-2

MISSION STATEMENT

We empower makers who use fabric and yarn
to make life more enjoyable.

CREDITS

PUBLISHER AND
CHIEF VISIONARY OFFICER
Jennifer Erbe Keltner

CONTENT DIRECTOR
Karen Costello Soltys

MANAGING EDITOR
Tina Cook

ACQUISITIONS EDITOR
Karen M. Burns

TECHNICAL EDITOR
Ellen Pahl

COPY EDITOR
Durby Peterson

DESIGN MANAGER
Adrienne Smitke

COVER AND
INTERIOR DESIGNER
Regina Girard

LOCATION PHOTOGRAPHER
Adam Albright

STUDIO PHOTOGRAPHER
Brent Kane

ILLUSTRATOR
Sandy Loi

SPECIAL THANKS

The photography for this book was taken at Lori Clark's The FarmHouse Cottage in Snohomish, Washington, and Whidbey Island Strawfield Farm Retreat, Greenbank, Washington. Both locations are available to rent through Airbnb..

Contents

Introduction

Growing up surrounded by three generations of handwork enthusiasts is what inspired my passion for creating. When I was a young child, I spent hours on end with my mother, Linda, and both my grandmother Avis and great grandmother Lily, who lived just up the hill from us out in the country. I was very fortunate to take part in many of their creative ventures, from going to ceramics classes with my mother to helping Lily braid wool rugs. I also spent hours sitting underneath the wooden quilt frame waiting (impatiently) to poke the yarn-threaded needle back up through the layers, so Avis could tie square knots on top of the quilt. Little did I know this would be the foundation for my creative journey!

While I was young, I played for hours in great grandma Lily's button box, and I enjoyed learning how to sew on her treadle sewing machine. She was so patient, and she loved helping me learn how to sew. Although the projects weren't much at the beginning, before I knew it I was picking out fabric and thread and beginning to sew projects to enter at the county fair through 4-H. I also loved to bake, garden, and dabble in many other creative pursuits offered by 4-H. I soon discovered I had a knack for creating, and I earned annual trips to the Minnesota State Fair by winning Grand Champion in several categories. This was a *big* deal, as the fair was seven hours away.

Fast forward to more recent years, and you will find me exploring more of the creative process. The quilting industry is where my passion currently lies. I *love* going outside the box by working with and combining different mediums and fibers, such as wool and cotton, in my work. I often mix embroidery with quilting and wool appliqué, for example. I also love to mix mediums to create a unique and textured look in my designs. Although wool is my favorite medium at the moment, it's just a small representation of my vintage-inspired look that many have come to know and appreciate.

Within these pages you will find an array of projects to adorn your home and hearth. You can use traditional embroidery stitches to create a wonderful embroidered wall hanging, use wool to make a sweet wool sheep pillow with woolen blankets, or simply use cotton fabrics to sew up a small quilt to grace your table. The designs in this book are versatile and can be made with ease. If you're new to wool, I hope you'll experiment with my tried-and-true wool-appliqué technique. It really makes working with wool a breeze! So get out those needles, dust off that sewing machine, and gather your wool—we have much creating to do!

~ Stacy

Summer Blooms PILLOW

FINISHED SIZE: 8½" × 8"

Materials

10" × 12" rectangle of beige linen for appliqué background

4" × 6" rectangle of green wool for stem

2" × 4" rectangle of pink wool for large flower

2" × 2" square of violet wool for small flower

1" × 2" rectangle of gold wool for butterfly body

1½" × 2" rectangle of purple wool for butterfly wing

3" × 4" rectangle of orange plaid wool for pot

1" × 4" rectangle of orange tweed wool for rim of pot

24 squares, 1½" × 1½", of assorted cotton prints for pieced side border

8½" × 9" rectangle of fabric for pillow back

¼ yard of lightweight 18"-wide fusible web

Embroidery floss in gold, green, orange, pink, purple, and violet

Fiberfill stuffing

Appliquéing the Design

1 Referring to "Wool Appliqué" on page 75, trace the patterns for the appliqués (page 9) onto the fusible web and prepare the wool shapes.

2 Referring to the photo on page 7 and the pattern for placement, fuse the pieces to the linen 10" × 12" background.

3 Use three strands of floss to blanket-stitch or whipstitch the pieces in place. On small pieces, you might prefer to use two strands of floss and a whipstitch. In the project shown, the flowerpot is stitched using the herringbone stitch (see "Embroidery Stitches" on page 77).

4 Add a few French knots and backstitches to add details to the butterfly's wing.

5 Trim the linen background to 6" × 8½", keeping the design centered.

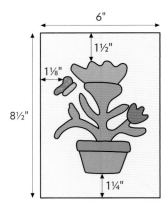

Tucking a small pillow or two in with other items is an easy way to enhance seasonal decor. This one is so sweet for summertime and it whips up in a jiffy! The pieced border of squares along the side is a nice addition and a fun way to add bits and pieces of your favorite prints.

2 Sew the checkerboard border to the left side of the linen appliquéd piece with right sides together. The unit should measure 8½" × 9", including seam allowances.

3 Right sides together, align the pillow front with the 8½" × 9" pillow back. Stitch the front and back together with a ¼" seam allowance, leaving a 2" opening to turn the pillow. Clip the corners and turn the pillow right side out.

Assembling the Pillow

Press the seam allowances after sewing each seam as indicated by the arrows in the diagrams.

1 To make the checkerboard side border, arrange and sew the squares together into eight rows of three squares each. Join the rows to make the side border, which should measure 3½" × 8½", including seam allowances.

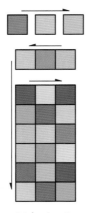

Make 1 unit,
3½" × 8½".

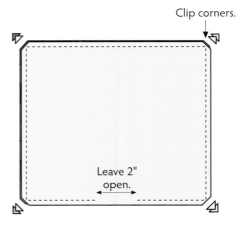

Clip corners.

Leave 2" open.

4 Stuff the pillow with fiberfill and stitch the opening closed.

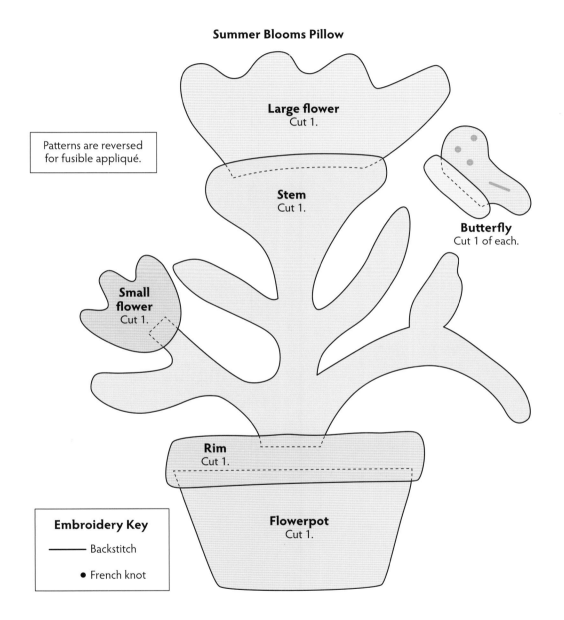

Summer Blooms Pillow

Patterns are reversed for fusible appliqué.

Large flower
Cut 1.

Stem
Cut 1.

Butterfly
Cut 1 of each.

Small flower
Cut 1.

Rim
Cut 1.

Flowerpot
Cut 1.

Embroidery Key

—— Backstitch

● French knot

Shoofly Pie MUG RUG

FINISHED MUG RUG: 13" × 8"

Materials

Fat quarters measure 18" × 21".

7" × 9" rectangle of tan solid for embroidery background

1 fat quarter of cheddar print for block and binding

4" × 10" rectangle of brown print for block

⅛ yard of orange print for sashing and border*

1 fat quarter of fabric for backing

12" × 17" piece of cotton batting

Embroidery floss in charcoal, gold, rose, variegated olive green, and violet

Black Pigma pen or other fine-point permanent marker

*The instructions are written for using one orange print in the sashing and border. Note that I used a different orange print for the right side border. Feel free to scrap it up!

Cutting

From the cheddar print, cut:
2 squares, 2⅞" × 2⅞"
4 squares, 2½" × 2½"
3 strips, 2½" × 21"

From the brown print, cut:
2 squares, 2⅞" × 2⅞"
1 square, 2½" × 2½"

From the orange print, cut:
2 strips, 1¼" × 42"; crosscut into:
• 2 strips, 1¼" × 11½"
• 2 strips, 1¼" × 8"
• 1 strip, 1¼" × 6½"

Stitching the Embroidered Block

1 Referring to "Embroidery" on page 76, trace the pattern on page 13 onto the tan rectangle using the permanent pen.

2 Stitch the design with three strands of floss using a backstitch, cross-stitch, French knot, and stem stitch as indicated on the pattern.

3 Press the block and trim to 4¾" × 6½".

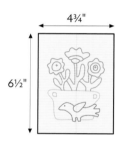

Making the Shoofly Block

Press the seam allowances after sewing each seam as indicated by the arrows in the diagrams.

1 Draw a diagonal line from corner to corner on the wrong side of each cheddar 2⅞" square. Right sides together, layer each cheddar square with a brown 2⅞" square. Sew ¼" from each side of the drawn line. Cut on the drawn line and press to make a total of four half-square-triangle units that measure 2½" square, including seam allowances.

Make 4 units.

10

Shoofly pie is a Pennsylvania German dessert made of molasses, eggs, flour, and brown sugar, baked in a pie crust. The colors of this mug rug evoke the sweet, dark brown pie alongside a fun and happy bouquet of hand-stitched flowers and a bird—the perfect place to rest your mug of coffee, tea, or cider.

2 Arrange the four cheddar 2½" squares, the half-square-triangle units, and the brown 2½" square as shown. Sew the squares into rows, and then join the rows to make the Shoofly block. The block should measure 6½" square, including seam allowances.

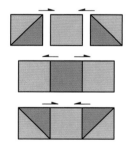

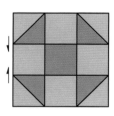

Make 1 block, 6½" × 6½".

Assembling the Mug Rug

For help with any of the following steps, go to ShopMartingale.com/HowtoQuilt for free, illustrated instructions.

1 Sew together the embroidered block and the Shoofly block, placing the orange 1¼" × 6½" strip between them.

2 Sew the orange 1¼" × 11½" strips to the top and bottom and press. Sew the orange 1¼" × 8" strips to the sides. The pieced top should measure 8" × 13".

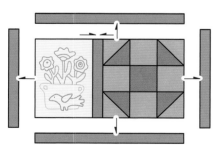

Mug rug assembly

3 Layer the top with the batting and backing. Baste the layers together and quilt. The mug rug shown is quilted in the ditch of the seams, with a meandering design around the embroidery.

4 Trim the batting and backing even with the top.

5 Using the cheddar 2½" × 21" strips, make and then attach the binding.

Shoofly Pie Mug Rug

Embroidery Key

——— Backstitch

✕ Cross-stitch

• French knot

--------- Stem stitch

Autumn PILLOW

FINISHED SIZE: 22" × 10½"

Materials

11" × 16½" rectangle of tan wool for background

6½" × 11" rectangle of brown plaid wool for
 side panel

3½" × 4" rectangle of burgundy wool for leaf
 sections and berries

8" × 17" rectangle of black wool for crow, pocket,
 sunflower center, and dogtooth border

4" × 4½" rectangle of gold wool for sunflower
 and moon

5" × 5" square of orange wool for leaves

4½" × 10½" rectangle of brown wool for branch,
 acorn, and sunflower center

2" × 6½" rectangle of brown tweed wool for
 crow's wing and acorn top

1¼" × 3¾" rectangle of green wool for pocket trim

3½" × 6½" rectangle of brown print for
 pocket backing

11" × 22½" rectangle of tan wool for pillow back

½ yard of 18"-wide lightweight fusible web

Embroidery floss or 12-weight pearl cotton in
 black, brown, burgundy, gold, orange, and tan

8 buttons, ¼" diameter, for crow's eye and
 sunflower center*

Fiberfill stuffing

*The project shown features sunflower seed
buttons, available from Buttermilk Basin. See
"Resources," page 79.

Appliquéing the Pillow Top

1 Referring to "Wool Appliqué" on page 75, trace
 the pattern for the dogtooth border (pattern
 sheet 1) onto the fusible web and prepare
 the border appliqué. Fuse it to the bottom
 of the tan 11" × 16½" wool rectangle,
 following the manufacturer's instructions.

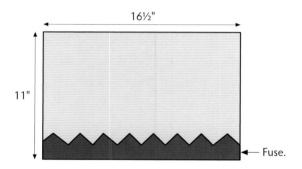

2 With right sides together and using a ¼"
 seam allowance, sew the tan 11" × 16½" wool
 rectangle to the brown plaid 6½" × 11" wool
 rectangle and press.

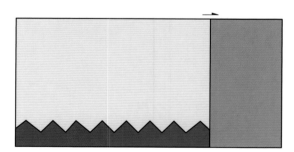

We love autumn at Buttermilk Basin. This darling pillow is perfect not only for fall but all year long. It's so fun to find sprigs or dried flowers to tuck in the pocket!

3. Trace the remaining appliqué shapes, including the pocket, onto the fusible web. Cut the fusible web shapes apart and adhere them to the chosen wool.

4. Cut out the wool shapes on the drawn lines. Refer to the illustration below and pattern sheet 1 for placement. Fuse all pieces to the background, except the pocket.

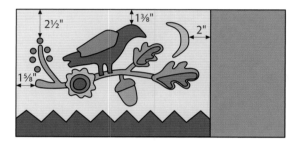

5. Before removing the paper backing from the pocket, fuse the pocket trim to the top of the pocket. Remove the paper backing and blanket-stitch the edges using three strands of floss or pearl cotton thread. Then embroider the stem using a feather stitch. Stitch French knots for the berries using six strands of floss.

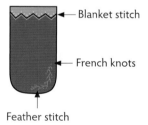

Blanket stitch

French knots

Feather stitch

6. Fuse the pocket to the wrong side of the brown print 3½" × 6½" rectangle. Trim the fabric even with the edges of the pocket. This gives the pocket a lining and adds stability.

7. Use three strands of floss or one strand of pearl cotton to blanket-stitch the appliqués in place on the background. On small pieces, you might prefer to use two strands of floss and a whipstitch.

8 Pin the pocket in place on the side panel, approximately 3½" down from the top and centered from side to side. Use floss and the blanket stitch to stitch around the pocket, leaving the top open.

Finishing

1 Use one strand of burgundy pearl cotton to feather stitch the wing details.

2 Sew a button in place for the crow's eye and seven buttons to the center of the sunflower.

3 Right sides together, layer the pillow top with the tan wool 11" × 22½" pillow back. Sew around the entire pillow, using a ¼" seam allowance and leaving a small opening at the bottom. Turn the pillow right side out, stuff the pillow with fiberfill, and whipstitch the opening closed. Find berries or dried flowers to tuck into the pocket!

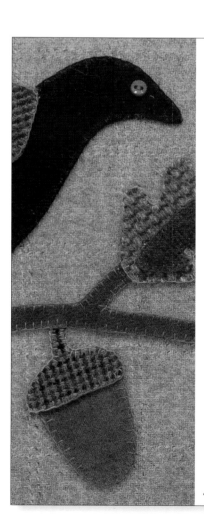

Dill Pickle Pasta Salad

Dill Pickle Pasta Salad is my daughter Hannah's favorite pasta salad. In this creamy recipe, dill pickles are the staple, adding great flavor and tons of crunch. This recipe is even better made ahead of time—it's the perfect potluck dish.

INGREDIENTS
½ pound dry shell pasta (about 3 cups)
½ cup dill pickle juice
¾ cup sliced dill pickles
⅔ cup cheddar cheese, diced
3 tablespoons white onion, finely diced
2 tablespoons fresh dill

DRESSING
⅔ cup mayonnaise
⅓ cup sour cream
⅛ teaspoon cayenne pepper
4 tablespoons dill pickle juice
Salt and pepper to taste

DIRECTIONS

1. Boil the pasta according to the package directions until al dente. Run under cold water to stop the cooking.

2. Toss the cold pasta with ½ cup of pickle juice and set aside for about 5 minutes. Drain and discard the pickle juice.

3. Combine all the dressing ingredients in a small bowl and mix well.

4. Toss all the ingredients in a large bowl. Refrigerate at least 1 hour before serving.

Hint of Fall QUILT

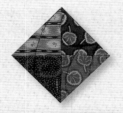

Materials

Yardage is based on 42"-wide fabric.

8 squares, 8" × 8", of assorted gold prints for blocks

8 squares, 8" × 8", of assorted black and/or brown prints for blocks (collectively referred to as "dark")

⅛ yard of gold print for inner border

⅜ yard of black print for outer border

¼ yard of black solid for binding

¾ yard of fabric for backing

26" × 27" piece of batting

Cutting

From *each* gold print square, cut:
1 rectangle, 3½" × 6" (8 total)
4 squares, 2" × 2" (32 total; 4 are extra)

From *each* dark print square, cut:
1 rectangle, 3½" × 6" (8 total; 1 is extra)
4 squares, 2" × 2" (32 total)

From the gold print for inner border, cut:
2 strips, 1" × 42"; crosscut into:
• 2 strips, 1" × 17"
• 2 strips, 1" × 16½"

From the black print, cut:
2 strips, 3" × 42"; crosscut *each* strip into:
• 1 strip, 3" × 21½" (2 total)
• 1 strip, 3" × 18" (2 total)

From the black solid, cut:
3 strips, 2½" × 42"

Assembling the Blocks

Press the seam allowances after sewing each seam as indicated by the arrows in the diagrams.

1. Draw a diagonal line from corner to corner on the wrong side of each 2" square.

2. For each gold 3½" × 6" rectangle, choose four matching 2" squares of one dark print.

3. Place a square on one corner as shown, aligning the raw edges. Stitch on the drawn line. Trim the seam allowances to ¼" and press.

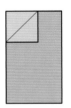 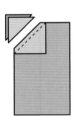 

4. Repeat step 3 on each corner to make a block measuring 3½" × 6", including seam allowances. Make eight blocks.

Make 8 blocks, 3½" × 6".

18

Dark, rich colors bring autumn to mind, but this assortment is just one of many color options to consider. Have fun making one quilt in fall hues, and then swap out the colors to sew another for each season.

2 Sew the gold print 1" × 17" strips to the sides of the quilt center. Sew the gold print 1" × 16½" strips to the top and bottom. The quilt center should measure 16½" × 18".

3 Sew the black 3" × 18" strips to the sides of the quilt. Sew the black 3" × 21½" borders to the top and bottom. The quilt should measure 21½" × 23".

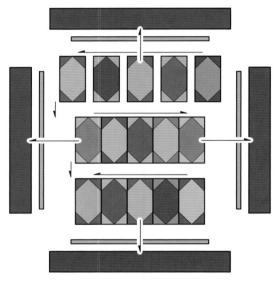

Quilt assembly

5 Repeat steps 2–4 with the dark rectangles and gold squares, but press the seam allowances toward the center. Make seven blocks.

Make 7 blocks,
3½" × 6".

Assembling the Quilt

1 Arrange the blocks in three rows of five blocks each, alternating the gold and dark centers. Sew the blocks into rows, and then join the rows to make the quilt center. The quilt center should measure 15½" × 17", including seam allowances.

Finishing

For help with any of the following steps, go to ShopMartingale.com/HowtoQuilt for free, illustrated instructions. Refer to "Adding a Hanging Sleeve" on page 78 if you want to hang your quilt.

1 Layer the quilt top with the batting and backing. Baste the layers together and quilt. The quilt shown is quilted in an allover design of loops and swirls in the center and a feathered vine in the outer border.

2 Trim the batting and backing even with the top.

3 Using the black 2½"-wide strips, make and then attach the binding.

Folk Art Heart PILLOW

Materials

12" × 15" rectangle of black wool for border, flowerpot, wing, and sunflower center

7" × 7" square of olive wool for stem

3½" × 3½" square of gold wool for leaves and flower base

4" × 4" square of gold plaid wool for sunflower

3" × 6" rectangle of brown-and-black tweed wool for sunflower center and crow

2½" × 4" rectangle of pink wool for flower

12" × 15" rectangle of tan wool for heart background

12" × 15" rectangle of dark wool for pillow back*

⅝ yard of lightweight 18"-wide fusible web

Embroidery floss or 12-weight pearl cotton in black, brown, gold, green, and pink

Valdani 12-weight Twisted Tweed gold-and-black pearl cotton

9 brown buttons, ¼" diameter, for sunflower center**

1 black button, ¼" diameter, for crow's eye

Fiberfill stuffing

Use a 12" × 15" piece of flannel or other fabric for the pillow back if you prefer.

**The project shown features sunflower seed buttons, available from Buttermilk Basin. See "Resources," page 79.*

Appliquéing the Pillow Top

1 Referring to "Wool Appliqué" on page 75, trace the patterns for the appliqués (pattern sheet 1) onto the fusible web and prepare the wool shapes.

2 Make a complete heart pattern and zigzag border pattern. Use the heart to cut the shape from the tan wool 12" × 15" rectangle. Trace the zigzag border onto fusible web and prepare the border using the black wool.

3 Referring to the illustration below and the pattern sheet for placement, fuse all of the appliqués, including the border, to the tan heart background.

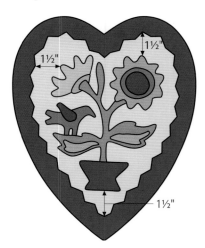

4 Use one strand of pearl cotton or three strands of floss to blanket-stitch the pieces in place. On small pieces, you might prefer to use one or two strands of floss and a whipstitch.

Both fun and functional, this heart pillow fits perfectly in the corner of your favorite chair. But I'm in love with dough bowls, and I'm hoping to find just the right bowl for displaying this heart! The thrill of the hunt is, of course, part of the fun.

Finishing

1. Stitch a grid as shown in the center of the sunflower with gold floss and straight stitches or a stem stitch. Sew the buttons to the center.

2. Sew a black button on the crow for an eye.

3. Use the heart pattern to cut a heart from the dark wool 12" × 15" rectangle for the pillow back.

4. Place the heart back and front right sides together and sew around the perimeter using a ¼" seam allowance and leaving a small opening on one side.

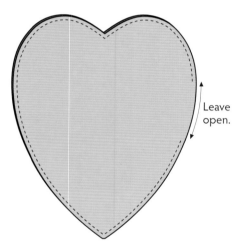

Leave open.

5. Clip the curves and turn right side out. Stuff firmly with fiberfill and whipstitch the opening closed.

6. Use the Twisted Tweed pearl cotton to feather stitch over the seam. Enjoy!

Cherry Cheesecake Dip

Cherry Cheesecake Dip is *sew* delicious! My friend Karen brought it to an event we did together at the shop, and it quickly became one of our party staples.

INGREDIENTS

1 box graham crackers
8 ounces cream cheese, softened
7 ounces marshmallow cream spread
16 ounces whipped dairy topping
42 ounces cherry pie filling
Vanilla wafers (optional)

DIRECTIONS

1. Crush one sleeve of graham crackers into tiny crumbs and place them in the bottom of a 9" × 13" pan, smoothing them to create an even layer.

2. Combine the softened cream cheese and the marshmallow cream in a bowl. Mix well. Stir the whipped dairy topping gently into the mixture.

3. Use a knife to gently spread the mixture over the graham cracker crumbs.

4. Top with cherry pie filling and chill until ready to serve.

5. Serve with the remaining graham crackers or vanilla wafers. A sure hit!

Olde Tyme PENNY MATS

It's amazing how the concept of the penny rug is still thriving, since it originated in the 1800s. I'm sure those amazing women never imagined designers would be keeping their traditions alive in the twenty-first century. Use your scraps on these fun mats and be thankful you don't have to back them with burlap bags or feed sacks as stitchers used to do!

Sheep Penny Mat

Both mats are made in the same way. Materials for the robins mat are on page 30.

Materials

2 squares, 9" × 9", of black wool for background and backing

2½" × 5" rectangle of cream wool for 3 sheep and 1 sheep's head

2" × 3" rectangle of gray wool for 1 sheep and 3 sheep heads

4" × 5" rectangle of gold wool for pineapples

2" × 3" rectangle of green wool for pineapple tops

⅜ yard of lightweight 18"-wide fusible web

Embroidery floss in black, brown, cream, gold, gray, and green

Valdani 12-weight Twisted Tweed black-and-cream pearl cotton

Appliquéing the Penny Mat

1 Referring to "Wool Appliqué" on page 75, trace the pattern for the scalloped circle (page 31) onto the fusible web and prepare the backing by fusing the web to one of the black wool 9" square pieces. Cut the scalloped circle along the traced lines.

2 Cut a second scalloped circle from black wool without the fusible web.

3 Trace the pattern for the sheep and pineapple on page 28 onto fusible web and prepare the wool pieces following the manufacturer's instructions.

4 Referring to the illustration below and the pattern for placement, arrange and fuse the pieces to the black wool circle without fusible web.

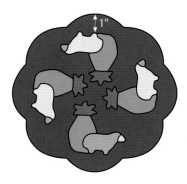

1"

5 Use three strands of floss to blanket-stitch the larger pieces in place. On small pieces, you might prefer to use one or two strands of floss and a whipstitch.

Embellishing and Finishing

Refer to "Embroidery Stitches" on page 77 as needed.

1 Use three strands of black floss to make a French knot on each sheep for the eye.

2 Use three strands of black floss to satin stitch an ear on the gray sheep and three strands of gray floss to stitch an ear on each of the other three sheep. Use three strands of gray floss and a chain stitch to stitch legs on each sheep.

3 Use one strand of green floss and straight stitches to create accent lines on the pineapple tops.

4 Use the Twisted Tweed pearl cotton to feather stitch around the perimeter of the mat about ¼" inside the scallops.

5 Place the stitched mat on top of the backing, aligning the edges. Fuse, following the manufacturer's instructions.

6 Using black floss, blanket-stitch the two pieces together around the perimeter.

Sheep Penny Mat

Patterns are reversed for fusible appliqué.

Sheep and pineapple
Cut 4 of each.

Embroidery Key

● French knot

⬯ Lazy daisy

◼ Satin stitch

— Straight stitch

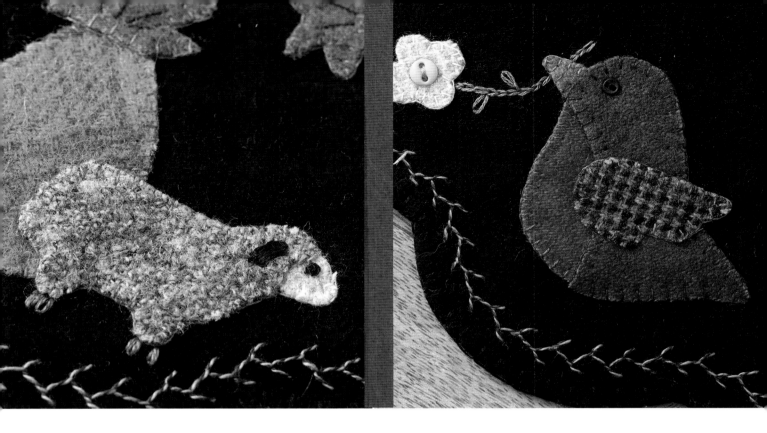

Jalapeño Popper Wonton Cups

Try a recipe that's a fun spin on the traditional jalapeño poppers.

INGREDIENTS
12 wonton wrappers
4 ounces cream cheese, softened
½ cup sour cream
12 ounces bacon, cooked and crumbled*
1 cup shredded cheddar cheese*
3 to 4 jalapeño peppers, seeded and chopped**

*Reserve 2 tablespoons for topping.
**For more heat, do not remove all the seeds.

DIRECTIONS
1. Preheat the oven to 350°.
2. Spray a muffin pan with cooking spray.
3. Place one wonton wrapper in each muffin cup; bake 8 minutes or until lightly browned.
4. Remove from the oven and cool slightly.
5. In a medium-sized mixing bowl, stir together the cream cheese, sour cream, bacon, cheddar cheese, and chopped jalapeños.
6. Spoon the filling into the wonton cups. Sprinkle with the reserved bacon and cheese.
7. Return the wonton cups to the oven and bake for an additional 8 to 10 minutes, until the wontons are golden brown and the cheese is melted.

Robins Penny Mat

Welcome spring by stitching this penny mat adorned with four perky robins.

Materials

2 squares, 9" × 9", of black wool for background and backing

5" × 6" rectangle of brown wool for robins

2½" × 4" rectangle of orange wool for breasts

1" × 2½" rectangle of gold wool for beaks

2½" × 3½" rectangle of brown plaid wool for wings

2" × 4" rectangle of cream wool for flowers

⅜ yard of lightweight 18"-wide fusible web

4 yellow buttons, ¼" diameter, for flower centers

4 tiny black buttons for robins' eyes

Embroidery floss in black, brown, cream, gold, green, and orange

Valdani 12-weight Twisted Tweed gold-and-black pearl cotton

Appliquéing the Penny Mat

Follow steps 1–5 for the Sheep Penny Mat on page 26, using the patterns for the robin and flower below.

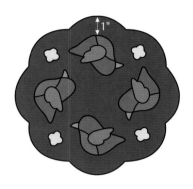

Finishing

Refer to "Embroidery Stitches" on page 77 if needed.

1   Sew a tiny black button on each robin for the eye and sew a yellow button in the center of each flower.

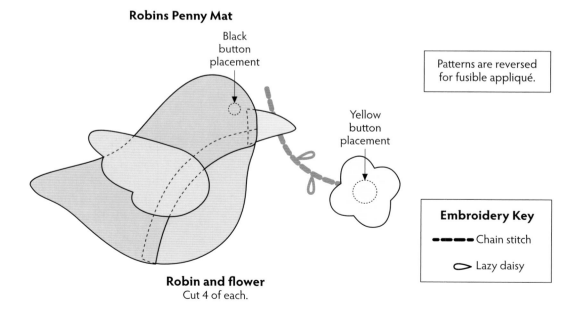

Robins Penny Mat

Black button placement

Patterns are reversed for fusible appliqué.

Yellow button placement

Robin and flower
Cut 4 of each.

Embroidery Key

- - - - Chain stitch

⟋ Lazy daisy

2 Use two strands of green floss to chain stitch the stem and leaves for each flower.

3 Use the Twisted Tweed pearl cotton to feather stitch around the perimeter of the mat about ¼" inside the scallops.

4 Place the stitched mat on top of the backing, aligning the edges. Fuse, following the manufacturer's instructions.

5 Using black floss, blanket-stitch the two pieces together around the perimeter.

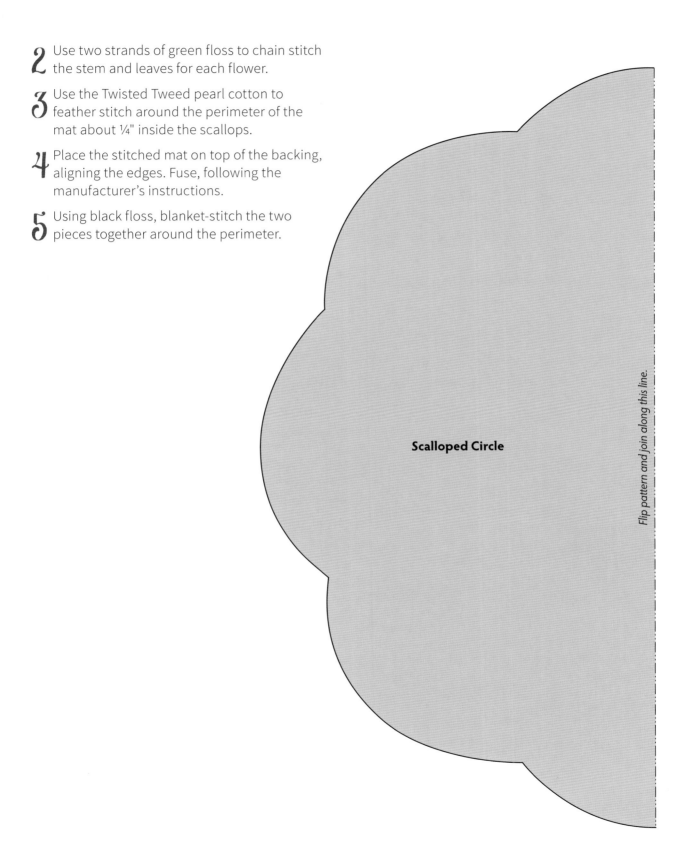

Scalloped Circle

Flip pattern and join along this line.

Sewing Jar QUILT

Materials

Yardage is based on 42"-wide fabric; fat eighths measure 9" × 21".

12" × 15" rectangle of cream solid for quilt center

¼ yard of cream print for Spool blocks

1 fat eighth *each* of dark tan solid and light tan solid for Spool blocks

14 squares, 1½" × 1½", of assorted prints for Spool blocks

¼ yard of black print for inner border

¼ yard of orange print for middle border

⅓ yard of brown print for outer border

¼ yard of burgundy print for binding

⅞ yard of fabric for backing

27" × 30" piece of batting

Embroidery floss in variegated black

Black Pigma pen or other fine-point permanent marker

Light box (optional)

Cutting

From the cream print, cut:
4 strips, 1½" × 42"; crosscut into 84 squares, 1½" × 1½"

From *each* tan solid, cut:
14 rectangles, 1½" × 3½" (28 total)

From the black print, cut:
2 strips, 1¾" × 42"; crosscut into:
- 2 strips, 1¾" × 18"
- 2 strips, 1¾" × 12½"

From the orange print, cut:
2 strips, 2¼" × 42"; crosscut *each* strip into:
- 1 strip, 2¼" × 21½" (2 total)
- 1 strip, 2¼" × 15" (2 total)

From the brown print, cut:
3 strips, 2¾" × 42"; crosscut into:
- 2 strips, 2¾" × 26"
- 2 strips, 2¾" × 18½"

From the burgundy print, cut:
3 strips, 2½" × 42"

Capture some old-fashioned charm with this embroidery canning jar quilt that's reminiscent of Grandma's old pincushion jar filled with sewing goodies. The embroidery is stitched with variegated black floss as a nod to the black floss that was often used years ago. Sweet Spool blocks complement the nostalgic mood.

Embroidering the Design

1. Copy the pattern on page 37 and place it between the cream solid 12" × 15" rectangle and a light box or window. Trace the pattern onto the cream fabric using the permanent pen.

2. Use three strands of black floss to embroider the design, referring to the embroidery key with the pattern. For smaller motifs such as the pins and thread, use two strands of floss.

3. After the stitching is complete, trim the block to 6½" × 9½", keeping the design centered.

Making the Spool Blocks

Press the seam allowances after sewing each seam as indicated by the arrows in the diagrams.

1. Draw a diagonal line from corner to corner on the wrong side of four cream 1½" squares. Right sides together, place a cream square on each end of a dark tan 1½" × 3½" rectangle as shown. Sew on the line and trim the seam allowances to ¼" to make the spool end unit. Make two units.

Make 2 units,
1½" × 3½".

Notice how the herringbone stitching around the embroidered block adds texture while also framing the handwork.

2 Sew a cream 1½" square to both sides of a print 1½" square to make the block center. Sew the units from step 1 together with the block center as shown. Make seven Spool blocks with dark tan and seven blocks with light tan. The blocks should measure 3½" square, including seam allowances.

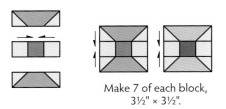

Make 7 of each block, 3½" × 3½".

Quilt Assembly

1 Arrange the Spool blocks around the embroidered quilt center, placing three blocks along the sides and four blocks along the top and bottom. Alternate the orientation of the blocks as shown in the quilt assembly diagram. Sew the blocks into two rows of three and two rows of four. Sew the three-block rows to the sides of the quilt center and then sew the four-block rows to the top and bottom. The quilt center should measure 12½" × 15½", including seam allowances.

2 Sew the black 1¾" × 12½" strips to the top and bottom of the quilt center. Sew the black 1¾" × 18" strips to the sides. The quilt center should measure 15" × 18", including seam allowances.

3 Sew the orange 2¼" × 15" strips to the top and bottom of the quilt center. Sew the orange 2¼" × 21½" strips to the sides. The quilt center should measure 18½" × 21½", including seam allowances.

4 Sew the brown 2¾" × 18½" strips to the top and bottom of the quilt. Sew the brown 2¾" × 26" strips to the sides. The quilt should measure 23" × 26".

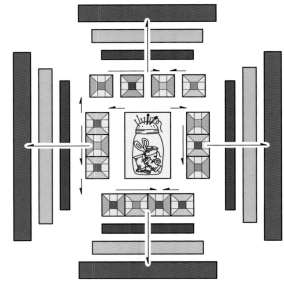

Quilt assembly

Finishing

For help with any of the following steps, go to ShopMartingale.com/HowtoQuilt for free, illustrated instructions. Refer to "Adding a Hanging Sleeve" on page 78 if you want to hang your quilt.

1 Using three strands of floss, stitch around the center block using a herringbone stitch over the seam.

2 Layer the quilt top with the batting and backing. Baste the layers together and quilt. The quilt shown is quilted in the ditch of the Spool blocks and with a meandering design around the embroidery. The inner border is quilted with spiral chain; the outer border features meander quilting.

3 Trim the batting and backing even with the top.

4 Using the burgundy 2½"-wide strips, make and then attach the binding.

Sewing Jar Quilt

Embroidery Key

—— Backstitch

✕ Cross-stitch

• French knot

■ Satin stitch

Woolly Sheep Pillow

FINISHED SIZE: 20" × 11"

Materials

20" × 26" rectangle of cream wool for sheep

6" × 14" rectangle of black wool for head and ear

Embroidery floss in black

Fiberfill stuffing

Button, ½" diameter, for eye

Making the Pillow

1 Cut out or trace the patterns for the sheep body, head, and ear (pattern sheet 2). Use the body pattern to cut two pieces from the cream wool. Using the patterns for the head and ear, cut two heads and one ear from the black wool.

2 Pin and then baste the head to the body along the placement line. Using three strands of black floss, blanket-stitch the head to the body and remove the basting stitches. Repeat for the second head and body pieces.

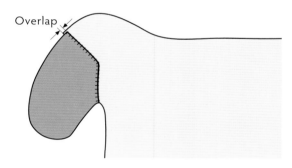

3 Pin or baste the ear in position on the body where indicated on the pattern. Use two strands of black floss to blanket-stitch the ear in place.

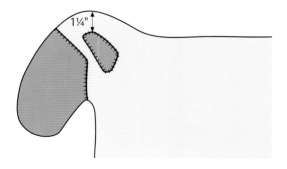

A cozy sheep pillow that's easy to stitch and big enough for cuddling is sure to bring a smile to all who see it. We've included three blanket options for the sheep here so he'll be sure to warm your heart each day of the year!

Blooming Flowers Blanket

FINISHED SIZE: 7¾" × 7½"

Materials

8½" × 8½" square of charcoal wool for foundation

7½" × 8" rectangle of tan wool for background

3" × 7" rectangle of burgundy plaid wool for center flower, star, and tongues

3" × 3" square of burgundy wool for base of center flower and circle flower

1" × 4" rectangle of aqua wool for flower stem and petiole

2" × 5" rectangle of olive wool for stems

1½" × 2½" rectangle of gold wool for leaf and circle flower's center

2" × 9" rectangle of aqua plaid wool for greenery and tongues

2" × 4½" rectangle of terra-cotta wool for vase

⅓ yard of lightweight 18"-wide fusible web

Embroidery floss in aqua, burgundy, charcoal, gold, olive green, tan, and terra-cotta

1 large gold seed bead for flower center

Finishing

1 Place the two sheep body pieces right sides together, aligning the edges. Pin and sew around the perimeter using a ¼" seam allowance and leaving a 3" to 4" opening along the bottom.

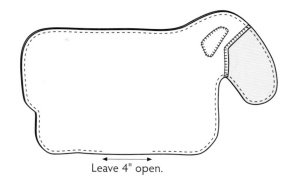

Leave 4" open.

2 Turn the pillow right side out and stuff with fiberfill. Whipstitch the opening closed.

3 Sew on a button for the eye.

4 Make one (or all!) of the blankets and attach it to the sheep with a few whipstitches to hold it in place. Remove the stitches with a seam ripper when you want to swap blankets.

Appliquéing the Blanket

1 Referring to "Wool Appliqué" on page 75, trace the patterns for the appliqués and tongue pieces (pattern sheet 2) onto the fusible web and prepare the wool appliqué pieces.

2 Make a pattern for the scalloped foundation and cut the foundation from the charcoal wool 8½" square.

3 Referring to the illustration below and the pattern sheet for placement, fuse all of the appliqués, including the tongue pieces, to the charcoal foundation.

Appliqué placement

4 Use two strands of floss to blanket-stitch the pieces in place. On small pieces, you might prefer to use two strands of floss and a whipstitch.

5 Blanket-stitch around the charcoal foundation using two strands of charcoal floss.

Embellishing and Finishing

1 Use two strands of charcoal floss to chain stitch the veins in the leaf.

2 Sew the gold bead in the center of the circle flower.

Watermelon Homestead Blanket

FINISHED SIZE: 7¾" × 7½"

Materials

8½" × 8½" square of black wool for foundation

4" × 8" rectangle of blue wool for sky

3" × 10" rectangle of cream herringbone wool for stripes and tongues

1½" × 8" rectangle of red wool for stripe

2½" × 6½" rectangle of dark red wool for watermelon

3" × 7" rectangle of light green wool for inner watermelon rind

3" × 7½" rectangle of green wool for watermelon rind

3" × 3" rectangle of gold plaid wool for large house

Continued on page 42

Continued from page 41

1½" × 2" rectangle of gold wool for small house

1" × 5" rectangle of black wool for roofs

1½" × 6" rectangle of red tweed wool for tongues

1" × 1" square of gray wool for chimneys

⅜ yard of lightweight 18"-wide fusible web

Embroidery floss in black, blue, cream, gold, green, red, and tan

7 large black seed beads for watermelon seeds (optional)

Appliquéing the Blanket

Follow steps 1–5 of "Appliquéing the Blanket" for the Blooming Flowers Blanket on page 40.

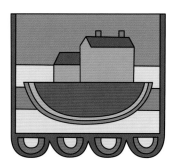

Appliqué placement

Embellishing and Finishing

1 Use six strands of tan floss to chain stitch the trunk of the tree on the left side of the house. Use two strands of green floss to chain stitch the limbs on the tree.

2 Use three strands of green floss to chain stitch the tree on the right.

3 Use three strands of black floss and the straight stitch to add the windows and doors to the house.

4 Sew black seed beads on the watermelon or satin stitch watermelon seeds using black floss.

Peanut Butter Corn-Chip Snack

Here's a snack that's so tasty and easy to make. Just break it up in chunks and enjoy!

INGREDIENTS

1 package corn chips

1 cup light corn syrup

1 cup sugar

1 cup creamy peanut butter

DIRECTIONS

1. Spread the corn chips on a greased cookie sheet.

2. In a saucepan over medium heat, bring the corn syrup and sugar to a boil, stirring frequently to help dissolve the sugar. Boil 1 minute. Remove from heat and stir in the peanut butter until smooth. Pour over the corn chips.

3. Allow to cool before devouring.

2" × 4" rectangle of black wool for crow and door

4" × 7" rectangle of green wool for flower stem

1" × 3" rectangle of light green wool for petioles

3½" × 5" rectangle of gold wool for flowers and tongues

⅓ yard of lightweight 18"-wide fusible web

Embroidery floss in black, burgundy, charcoal, gold, gray, green, and tan

1 small silver seed bead for crow's eye

Appliquéing the Blanket

Follow steps 1–5 of "Appliquéing the Blanket" for the Blooming Flowers Blanket on page 40.

Appliqué placement

Homestead in the Flowers Blanket

FINISHED SIZE: 7¾" × 7½"

Materials

8½" × 8½" square of charcoal wool for foundation

7½" × 8" rectangle of tan wool for background

3" × 8" rectangle of burgundy plaid wool for house and tongues

1½" × 3½" rectangle of taupe wool for roof

1½ " × 2" rectangle of gray wool for chimneys and bird wing

Embellishing and Finishing

1 Use six strands of black floss and a straight stitch to create the windows on the house.

2 Sew the silver seed bead on the crow.

Maple Leaf QUILT

FINISHED QUILT: 21½" × 21½" • FINISHED BLOCK: 4" × 4"

Materials

Yardage is based on 42"-wide fabric.

½ yard of brown print for blocks and outer border

¼ yard of beige print for blocks and inner border

4" × 7" rectangle of gold print for blocks

¼ yard of orange print for setting blocks

¼ yard of orange tone on tone for binding

¾ yard of fabric for backing

26" × 26" piece of batting

Cutting

From the brown print, cut:

1 strip, 1½" × 42"

2 strips, 4½" × 42"; from *each* strip, cut:
  • 1 strip, 4½" × 21½" (2 total)
  • 1 strip, 4½" × 13½" (2 total)

2 squares, 2⅞" × 2⅞"; cut in half diagonally to make 4 triangles

From the beige print, cut:

4 squares, 2⅞" × 2⅞"; cut in half diagonally to make 8 triangles

1 strip, 1½" × 42"

2 strips, 1" × 42"; crosscut into:
  • 2 strips, 1" × 13½"
  • 2 strips, 1" × 12½"

From the gold print, cut:

2 squares, 2⅞" × 2⅞"; cut in half diagonally to make 4 triangles

From the orange print, cut:

5 squares, 4½" × 4½"

From the orange tone on tone, cut:

3 strips, 2½" × 42"

Making the Blocks

Press the seam allowances after sewing each seam as indicated by the arrows in the diagrams.

1. Sew a brown triangle to a beige triangle to make a half-square-triangle unit. Make four units that measure 2½" square, including seam allowances. Repeat with the gold triangles and beige triangles to make four units.

Make 4 units of each, 2½" × 2½".

2. Sew the beige 1½" × 42" strip to the brown 1½" × 42" strip to make a strip set. Cut 16 segments, 1½" wide.

1½"

Make 1 strip set.
Cut 16 segments.

In Minnesota we love the four seasons, and autumn is an especially beautiful time of year. One can only imagine how many maple leaves fall, and this darling quilt captures some of their gorgeous colors.

3 Sew two segments together to make a four-patch unit. Make eight units that measure 2½" square, including seam allowances.

Make 8 units,
2½" × 2½".

4 Arrange and sew two matching half-square-triangle units and two four-patch units as shown. Make a total of four blocks that measure 4½" square, including seam allowances.

Make 2 of each block,
4½" × 4½".

Assembling the Quilt

1 Referring to the quilt assembly diagram, arrange the blocks and orange 4½" squares in three rows of three blocks each. Sew the blocks into rows and then join the rows to make the quilt center. The quilt center should measure 12½" square, including seam allowances.

2 Sew the beige 1" × 12½" strips to the sides of the quilt center. Sew the beige 1" × 13½" strips to the top and bottom. The quilt center should measure 13½" square, including seam allowances.

3 Sew the brown 4½" × 13½" strips to the sides of the quilt. Sew the brown 4½" × 21½" strips to the top and bottom.

Finishing

For help with any of the following steps, go to ShopMartingale.com/HowtoQuilt for free, illustrated instructions. Refer to "Adding a Hanging Sleeve" on page 78 if you want to hang your quilt.

1 Layer the quilt top with the batting and backing. Baste the layers together and quilt. The quilt shown is quilted with maple leaves connected by loops and swirls.

2 Trim the batting and backing even with the top.

3 Using the orange 2½"-wide strips, make and then attach the binding.

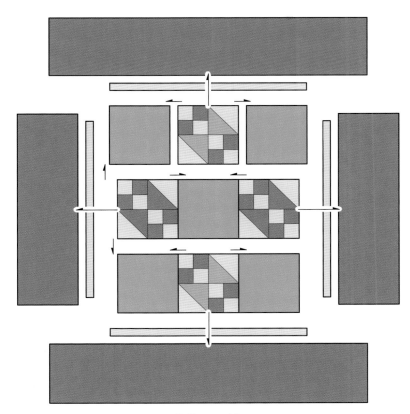

Quilt assembly

Seasons in Blackwork QUILT

Enjoy the best of what each month has to offer, from snowmen and mittens to birds and blooms to festive pumpkins and candy canes. Start embroidering these fun designs in the New Year and you could be finished by Valentine's Day, or stitch one block a month to savor the stitching all year long.

Materials

Yardage is based on 42"-wide fabric.

1⅓ yards of cream tone on tone for block backgrounds and middle border

1⅓ yards of black print for sashing, borders, and binding

1⅜ yards of fabric for backing

39" × 46" piece of batting

Embroidery floss in black

Black Pigma pen or other fine-point permanent marker

Cutting

From the cream tone on tone, cut:

3 strips, 12" × 42"; cut into 12 rectangles, 8" × 12"
4 strips, 1½" × 42"; cut into:
- 2 strips, 1½" × 28½"*
- 2 strips, 1½" × 23½"*
- 6 squares, 1½" × 1½"

From the black print, cut:

8 strips, 1½" × 42"; cut into:
- 2 strips, 1½" × 26½"*
- 2 strips, 1½" × 21½"*
- 9 rectangles, 1½" × 8½"
- 8 rectangles, 1½" × 4½"
4 strips, 5" × 42"; cut into:
- 2 strips, 5" × 32½"*
- 2 strips, 5" × 30½"*
4 strips, 2½" × 42"

Note that these are the mathematically correct border measurements. It's always best to measure the actual width and length of your quilt through the center before cutting borders; measurements may vary depending on your seam allowances.

Embroidering the Blocks

1 Referring to "Embroidery" on page 76, trace the 12 patterns (pattern sheet 3) onto the cream 8" × 12" rectangles using the permanent pen.

2 Use the backstitch or chain stitch and three to five strands of black floss to stitch the outlines, referring to the embroidery key with each pattern. Use two to three strands of floss for the smaller details. Refer to "Embroidery Stitches" on page 77 and feel free to use different stitches if you prefer.

3 After completing the embroidery, press and trim each block to 4½" × 8½", keeping the designs centered.

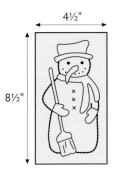

4½"

8½"

Assembling the Quilt

Press the seam allowances after sewing each seam as indicated by the arrows in the diagrams.

1 Arrange the blocks in three rows of four blocks each, placing the black 1½" × 8½" sashing rectangles between the blocks. Sew the blocks into rows.

2 Sew four black 1½" × 4½" sashing rectangles together with three cream 1½" squares to make a horizontal sashing row. Make two rows.

3 Sew the block rows and sashing rows together to make the quilt center. The quilt center should measure 19½" × 26½", including seam allowances.

4 Sew the black 1½" × 26½" strips to the sides of the quilt center. Sew the black 1½" × 21½" strips to the top and bottom. The quilt center should measure 21½" × 28½", including seam allowances.

5 Sew the cream 1½" × 28½" strips to the sides of the quilt center. Sew the cream 1½" × 23½" strips to the top and bottom. The quilt center should measure 23½" × 30½", including seam allowances.

6 Sew the black 5" × 30½" strips to the sides of the quilt. Sew the black 5" × 32½" strips to the top and bottom. The quilt should measure 32½" × 39½".

Finishing

For help with any of the following steps, go to ShopMartingale.com/HowtoQuilt for free, illustrated instructions. Refer to "Adding a Hanging Sleeve" on page 78 if you want to hang your quilt.

1 Layer the quilt top with the batting and backing. Baste the layers together and quilt. The quilt shown is quilted with a diagonal grid in the center and a feathered vine in the outer border.

2 Trim the batting and backing even with the top.

3 Using the black 2½"-wide strips, make and then attach the binding.

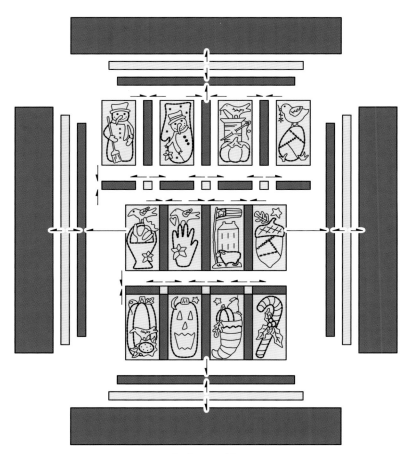

Quilt assembly

Crazy-Stitched Pineapple MAT

Materials

Fat quarters measure 18" × 21".

3 rectangles, 4" × 5", of assorted green wools for pineapple top

5 rectangles, 4" × 6", 5" × 6", 4" × 5", 2" × 5", and 3" × 6", of assorted gold wools for pineapple

3" × 4" rectangle of black wool for moon, star, and door

3" × 4" rectangle of black tweed wool for roof

5½" × 10" rectangle of brown wool for tree

6" × 7" rectangle of red wool for house

2¼" × 4¼" rectangle of green plaid wool for grass

2½" × 7" rectangle of green wool for grass

1 fat quarter of muslin for foundation

12" × 18" rectangle of wool for backing*

⅔ yard of lightweight 18"-wide fusible web

Embroidery floss or 12-weight pearl cotton in brown, gold, green, and red

Embroidery floss in black

*Optional; use flannel or cotton for backing if you prefer.

Appliquéing the Pineapple

1 Referring to "Wool Appliqué" on page 75, trace the patterns for the pineapple and appliqués (pattern sheet 1) onto the fusible web, roughly cut them out and adhere the patterns to the appropriate wools following the manufacturer's instructions.

2 Cut out the wool shapes on the drawn lines.

3 Trace the patterns for the pineapple and interior pieces onto paper. Turn the paper over and trace that pattern to get a reversed design. Use this to trace the design onto the muslin foundation for a placement guide. Save the paper pattern to use when cutting the backing.

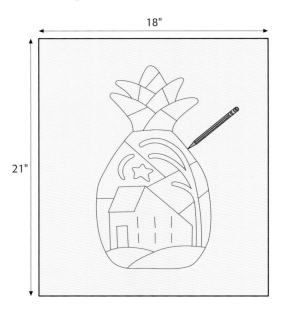

4 Following the placement guide, arrange the pieces on the muslin foundation, assembling the pineapple like a puzzle. Begin at the top and work downward, adding the grass last. Fuse all pieces to the muslin background.

5 Trim the excess muslin so that it's even with the wool.

Welcome your guests with a crazy-stitched pineapple mat. Pineapples traditionally represent warmth, welcome, friendship, and hospitality. The decorative stitching enhances the piece and offers the perfect opportunity to learn and practice new stitches.

Stitching and Embellishing

The stitching, which is both decorative and functional, is done with Valdani 12-weight pearl cotton using colors that both coordinate and contrast with the wool patches. I wanted the stitching to show up nicely as part of the design. There are no limits to the types of embroidery stitches you can use. See "Embroidery Stitches" on page 77 for basic stitches or use your favorite. Get creative and have fun with the stitching—you can't go wrong!

1 Using pearl cotton or three strands of floss, stitch along the "seams" of all the background patches in the pineapple top and base. I used a feather stitch, cross-stitch, and lazy daisy stitch in groups of three to create flower shapes.

2 Use two strands of black floss to chain stitch windows on the side of the house.

3 Use pearl cotton or three strands of floss to blanket-stitch the house pieces, tree, star, moon, and grass in place. On small pieces, you might prefer to use one to two strands of floss and a whipstitch.

Finishing

1 Use the paper pattern to cut a backing piece from wool or flannel.

2 Wrong sides together, layer the backing with the pineapple front. Pin together and blanket-stitch around the entire design using coordinating pearl cotton.

Bacon Ranch Cheese Ball

Who doesn't love bacon in a cheese ball? This cheese ball is so quick and easy to make, it'll be a big hit at your next party!

INGREDIENTS
8 ounces cream cheese, softened
½ cup sour cream
1 teaspoon dried parsley flakes
¼ teaspoon salt
½ teaspoon dried chives
¼ teaspoon oregano
¼ teaspoon tarragon
¼ teaspoon garlic powder
¼ teaspoon lemon pepper
½ cup bacon, fried and chopped

DIRECTIONS
1. Place all ingredients except the bacon in a bowl and mix well.

2. Scoop the cheese mixture out of the bowl and shape into a ball. Gently roll the ball in the bacon.

3. Wrap the cheese ball in plastic wrap and chill until ready to serve.

Ball Jar WALL HANGING

Handwork is free therapy if you ask me! When I pick up a needle, all thoughts of the day's troubles drift away and I relax as the needle finds its rhythm. When you need something to stitch away the blues, consider stitching a Ball canning jar and sewing motifs either in wool or embroidery. *Sew* good for the soul, I say!

Materials

Yardage is based on 42"-wide fabric; fat quarters measure 18" × 21".

6" × 13" rectangle of black wool for appliqué background

5" × 6½" rectangle of blue gray wool for jar

1¼" × 4" rectangle of olive wool for pincushion tops

1" × 2" rectangle of brown wool for spool end

1" × 2" rectangle of cream wool for needle

3" × 4½" rectangle of brown tweed wool for scissors and jar lid

3" × 4" rectangle of pink wool for thread, middle section of tomato, and strawberry

2½" × 3½" rectangle of raspberry wool for tomato

⅛ yard of pink print for border

¼ yard of black solid for binding

1 fat quarter of fabric for backing

12" × 19" piece of batting

¼ yard of 18"-wide lightweight fusible web

Embroidery floss in black, brown, gray, olive green, and pink

12-weight pearl cotton in variegated pink

3 assorted buttons, ⅜" to ⅝" diameter, for embellishment

Cutting

From the pink print, cut:
1 strip, 1¾" × 42"; crosscut into:
- 2 strips, 1¾" × 12"
- 2 strips, 1¾" × 7½"

From the black solid, cut:
2 strips, 2½" × 42"

Appliquéing the Design

1. Referring to "Wool Appliqué" on page 75, trace the patterns for the appliqués (on page 59) onto the fusible web and prepare the wool shapes.

2. Referring to the photo on page 57 and the pattern for placement, fuse the pieces to the black wool 6" × 13" background.

3. Use three strands of floss to blanket-stitch the pieces in place. On small pieces, you might prefer to use two strands of floss and a whipstitch.

Embellishing

1. Use three strands of pink floss to stem stitch the thread on the scissors and needle.

2. Use three strands of black floss to chain stitch the word *Ball* on the jar. Use a stem stitch for the lines on the jar lid and the pins on the pincushion.

3. Use three strands of olive green floss to stem stitch the string from the top of the pincushion to the berry.

Assembling the Quilt

Press the seam allowances after sewing each seam as indicated by the arrows in the diagrams.

1. Trim the wool appliquéd piece to 5" × 12".

2. Sew the pink 1¾" × 12" strips to the sides of the appliquéd piece. Sew a pink 1¾" × 7½" strip to the top and bottom. The quilt should measure 7½" × 14½".

3. Using the variegated pink pearl cotton, feather stitch over the wool and cotton seams.

Wall-hanging assembly

Finishing

For help with any of the following steps, go to ShopMartingale.com/HowtoQuilt for free, illustrated instructions. Refer to "Adding a Hanging Sleeve" on page 78 if you want to hang your quilt.

1. Layer the quilt top with the batting and backing. Baste the layers together and quilt. The quilt shown is quilted with a meandering design in the border.

2. Trim the batting and backing even with the top.

3. Using the black 2½"-wide strips, make and then attach the binding.

4. Sew the three buttons on the string for the finishing touch.

Patterns are reversed
for fusible appliqué.

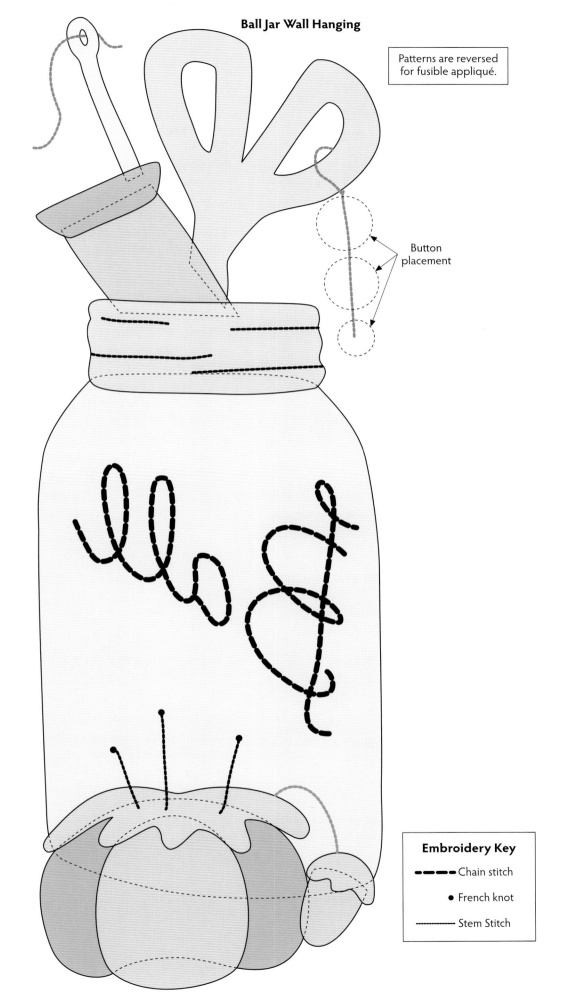

Button
placement

Embroidery Key

▬ ▬ ▬ ➤ Chain stitch

● French knot

┈┈┈┈ Stem Stitch

Ball Jar in Stitches

FINISHED WALL HANGING: 9" × 16"

MATERIALS

Yardage is based on 42"-wide fabric; fat quarters measure 18" × 21".

8" × 15" rectangle of cream solid for embroidery background

¼ yard of blue print for border

¼ yard of red print for binding

1 fat quarter of fabric for backing

13" × 20" piece of batting

Embroidery floss in charcoal, gray, green, and red*

3 assorted buttons, ⅜" to ½" diameter, for embellishment

Brown or black Pigma pen or other fine-point permanent marker

The project shown features Variegated Valdani (O775 and O501) and Weeks Dye Works (1222 for the needle) 6-strand floss.

CUTTING

From the blue print, cut:

2 strips, 2½" × 42"; crosscut into:
 • 2 strips, 2½" × 12"
 • 2 strips, 2½" × 9"

From the red print, cut:

2 strips, 2½" × 42"

EMBROIDERING THE DESIGN

1. Referring to "Embroidery" on page 76, trace the pattern on page 61 onto the cream 8" × 15" background using the permanent pen.

2. Use three strands of floss for all stitching. Chain stitch the word *Ball* on the jar and embroider French knots on the strawberry. Use a backstitch or stem stitch for all of the other stitching.

3. After the stitching is complete, press carefully and trim to 5" × 12", keeping the design centered.

ASSEMBLING AND FINISHING THE QUILT

Press the seam allowances after sewing each seam as indicated by the arrows in the diagrams. For help with any of the following steps, go to ShopMartingale.com/HowtoQuilt for free, illustrated instructions. Refer to "Adding a Hanging Sleeve" on page 78 if you want to hang your quilt.

1. Sew the blue 2½" × 12" strips to the sides of the stitched center. Sew the blue 2½" × 9" strips to the top and bottom.

Wall hanging assembly

2. Layer the quilt top with the batting and backing. Baste the layers together and quilt. The quilt shown is quilted with a pebble design around the embroidery and a chain of loops in the border.

3. Trim the batting and backing even with the top.

4. Using the red 2½"-wide strips, make and then attach the binding.

5. Sew the three buttons on the string and enjoy!

Embroidery Key

——— Back stitch

▬▬▬▬▬ Chain stitch

● French knot

Button placement

Crow's Harvest PILLOW

Materials

12" × 15" rectangle of tan wool for pillow front (appliqué background)

4" × 8" rectangle of black wool for crow

2" × 3½" rectangle of gray wool for crow's wing

1½" × 3½" rectangle of green wool for pumpkin stem

1½" × 2" rectangle *each of 3* gold wools for leaves

5" × 7" rectangle of orange wool for pumpkin and berries

3" × 4" rectangle of brown tweed wool for pumpkin accents

9" × 12½" rectangle of wool or other fabric for pillow back

Scraps of yellow and pale orange wool for berries

¼ yard of lightweight 18"-wide fusible web

Embroidery floss in black, brown, gold, gray, olive green, and orange

Tiny black button for crow's eye

Fiberfill stuffing

Appliquéing the Pillow Top

1 Referring to "Wool Appliqué" on page 75, trace the patterns for the appliqués (page 65) onto the fusible web and prepare the wool shapes. You can simply cut the berries freehand without fusible web if you like.

2 Referring to the photo on page 63 and the pattern for placement, fuse all of the pieces except the berries to the tan wool 12" × 15" background.

3 Use two or three strands of floss to blanket-stitch or whipstitch the pieces in place.

Embellishing

1 Use three strands of brown floss and a stem stitch to embroider the stem in the crow's mouth.

2 Stitch the berries in place with a French knot in the center of each.

3 Use two or three strands of olive green floss for the fly stitch in the leaves.

4 Use black floss to stitch the details in the crow's wing with a stem stitch and French knots. Add the button for the crow's eye.

Sometimes simplicity is best! Use wool with a homespun look for the background to create an instantly aged quality. A simple French knot holds each bittersweet berry in place, giving the design a fun dimensional effect.

5 Trim the pillow front to 9" × 12½", keeping the design centered.

6 Using three strands of black floss, stitch a running stitch 1¼" from the outer edges of the pillow.

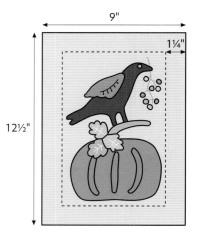

Assembling the Pillow

1 Right sides together, layer the pillow front and the 9" × 12½" back. Using a ¼" seam allowance, sew the pillow front and back together around the edges, leaving a 2" opening along the bottom to turn and stuff the pillow.

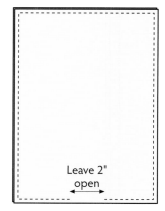

Leave 2" open

2 Clip the corners and turn the pillow right side out. Stuff with fiberfill and stitch the opening closed.

Crow's Harvest Pillow

Button placement

Patterns are reversed for fusible appliqué.

Embroidery Key

>>>> Fly stitch

● French knot

------- Stem stitch

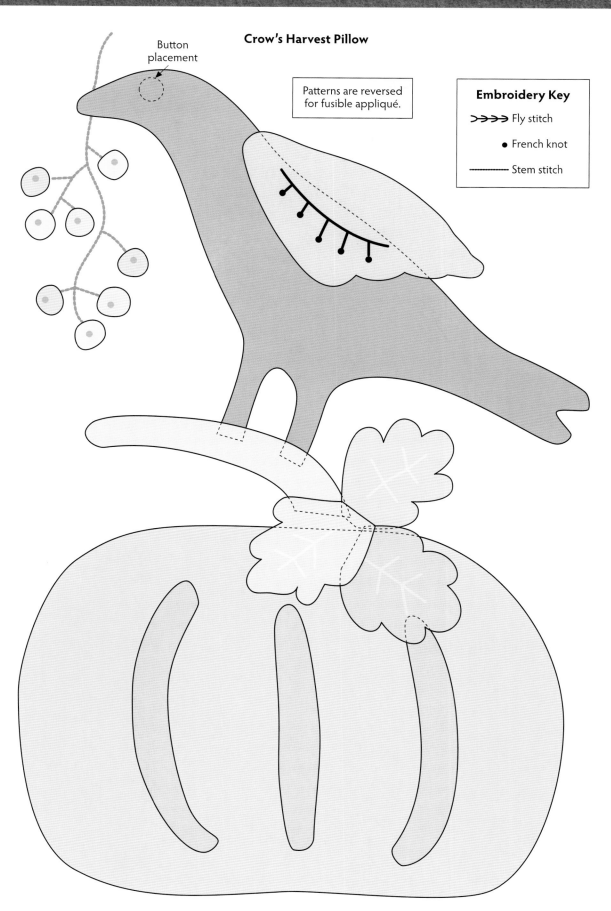

Sheltering Tree PICTURE

Materials

8½" × 8½" square of tan wool for background

10" × 10" square of black wool for zigzag border

4" × 6" rectangle of gold plaid wool for pineapple

2" × 2½" rectangle of olive wool for inner pineapple top

3" × 6" rectangle of green wool for outer pineapple top and leaves

1" × 4" rectangle of brown wool for tree trunk

3" × 4" rectangle of cream tweed wool for sheep

1½" × 3½" rectangle of black wool for sheep's head, ear, and feet

1½" × 1½" rectangle of red wool for star

14" × 14" square of brown plaid wool for background

½ yard of lightweight 18"-wide fusible web

Embroidery floss or 12-weight pearl cotton in brown, black, cream, red, and green

14" × 14" piece of lightweight batting

16½" × 16½" black wood frame with 10" × 10" opening

Appliquéing the Design

1 Referring to "Wool Appliqué" on page 75, trace the patterns for the appliqués and zigzag background (pages 69 and 70) onto the fusible web and prepare the wool shapes.

2 Referring to the photo on page 67 and the pattern for placement, fuse the pieces to the tan wool 8½" background square.

3 Use three strands of floss or one strand of pearl cotton to blanket-stitch the pieces in place. On small pieces, you might prefer to use two strands of floss and a whipstitch.

Embellishing

1 Use three strands of brown floss and a stem stitch to embroider the branches of the tree.

2 Use three strands of black floss to feather stitch lines on the pineapple top.

3 Use six strands of cream floss to make a French knot on the sheep for an eye.

4 Use three strands of green floss to add a straight stitch or a couple backstitches to each leaf.

5 Trim and square up the piece to 8" square.

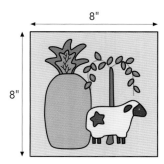

A primitive frame shows off a darling wool block, but there are other options too. Turn the block into a table mat or pillow, quilt it, or incorporate it into a larger wall hanging. The images in the design are classic and charming—have fun with your Sheltering Tree!

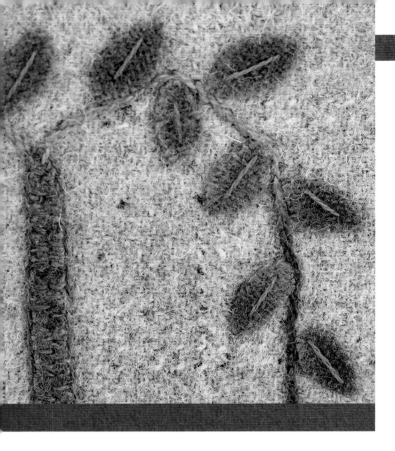

3 Center and fuse the tan wool piece to the black zigzag piece.

4 Use three strands of coordinating floss to blanket-stitch the tan background to the black zigzag piece. Blanket-stitch the black zigzag section to the brown plaid background.

5 Place the piece right side down on a flat surface and align the 14" square of batting on top. Place the cardboard insert from the frame on top, centering it over the batting and wool. (Note that you will need to create a 10" square cardboard insert if your frame did not come with one.)

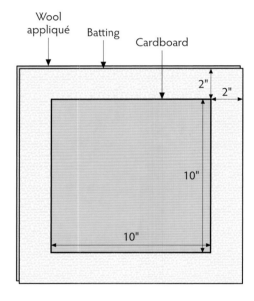

Finishing

1 Center the black zigzag wool piece on the brown plaid 14" wool square and fuse in place.

2 Cut two strips of fusible web that are a scant 1" × 6" and two strips that are a scant 1" × 8". Fuse these along the edges on the wrong side of the stitched tan wool piece.

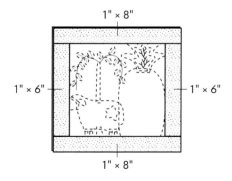

6 Fold the excess wool and batting over the cardboard and tape to secure it in place.

7 Insert the cardboard into the frame and replace the frame backing.

Sheltering Tree Picture

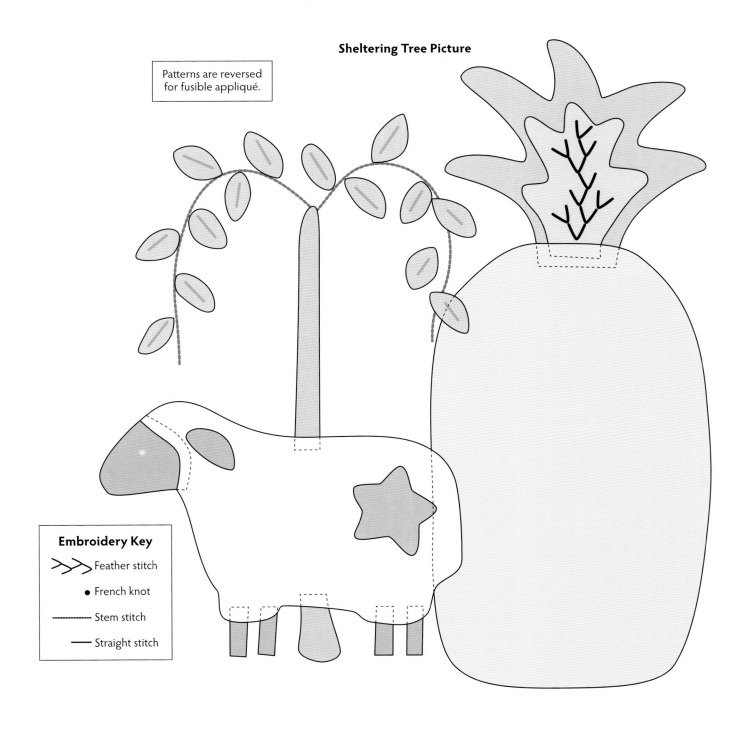

Patterns are reversed
for fusible appliqué.

Embroidery Key

>>> Feather stitch

● French knot

-------- Stem stitch

—— Straight stitch

Zigzag background
Cut 1.

Background
placement

Flip pattern and join along this line.

Wool Appliqué, Embroidery, AND MORE

As you have probably gathered by now, wool is my favorite medium to work in! There's something about wool that brings joy to my heart. I think my passion for it stems from growing up with generations of family members, including my great-grandparents. During the long winters here in Minnesota, there never was a day that great-grandma Lily wasn't donning her wool coat and fur hat, while many of the men in the family sported buffalo plaid wool hats and coats. Over the years, wool has remained constant in an ever-changing world, making it a traditional staple in the handwork community.

Although I would never cut into my great-grandmother's wool coat, many stitchers do glean wool from old coats. I prefer to work with my line of wool from Henry Glass and a few select hand-dyed wool pieces from various artists. When I was designing my line of wool for Henry Glass, I wanted to create a palette that was reminiscent of the vintage colors that were often seen back in the day. I also wanted to make sure it was 100% wool, so it's perfect for artists who want to overdye and for those of us who prefer to felt it up. Working with 100% wool is always your best option, but I would never pass up a fabulous piece simply because it was a blend.

I also feel it's important to incorporate various textures or styles of wool into my work. Therefore, I made sure to include gorgeous plaids and herringbone patterns in my line. These really bring dimension to projects. They also add a nice contrast to the solid pieces of wool and allow you to make certain pieces pop; try switching to a textured piece of wool in the same color. Giving dimension to your work makes it more appealing to the eye, so never be afraid to mix and match!

Add texture by using patterned wool.

Types of Wool

There are three types of wool used for wool appliqué. The first is vintage or repurposed wool; the second is new, off-the-bolt wool; and the third is hand-dyed wool. You can use any of these options for the projects in this book. At Buttermilk Basin, we use 100% wool in our projects. The only time I make an exception is when I stumble upon a fabulous vintage piece and just have to use it, even though it may not be 100% wool.

Vintage or repurposed wool. You may recall your grandmother wearing wool skirts years ago. Those skirts tend to be lighter weight wool, but they offer unique textures and colors. They would be perfect to felt and use in your projects. You may also remember those gorgeous wool army blankets that got much use over the years. Those are heavier weight and would work best for backgrounds or to make into Christmas stockings. Many wool items for repurposing can be found at thrift stores or estate sales. If you choose to work with vintage wool, just be sure that it's clean, 100% wool. Felt it as necessary prior to using it in your projects.

New, off-the-bolt wool. This is any new wool available in your local quilt shop or online, such as my line with Henry Glass. It can usually be found in two widths, 45" or 52". The width varies by manufacturer. This type can be found in many colors, textures, and weights, from suit weight to coat weight. When purchasing our wool or any wool from a bolt, you will need to felt it prior to using it in your projects, just like vintage wool. See "Felting Wool" on page 73 for directions.

Hand-dyed wool. Hand-dyed wool is stunning! There is simply no other way to describe it. The artist starts out with a piece of vintage or bolt wool and mixes dyes, water, and vinegar to create a one-of-a-kind piece of wool. During the dye process the wool also gets felted, so you do not have to felt hand-dyed wool after your purchase. Since vinegar is used in this process, the wool also becomes colorfast, making it perfect to use in any project! These pieces of wool are often mottled and you can see many different colors within one piece, which makes it fun to work with. One of the downsides to hand-dyed wool is that each piece is unique, making it difficult to recreate if you need or want more. Another downside is that the process is time consuming, so the wool tends to be expensive. Regardless, I never pass up a unique piece of wool to add to my stash!

Repurposed wool. Notice the sleeve shapes and once-upon-a-time darts.

Mottled and overdyed plaid wool can create one-of-a-kind looks.

Felting Wool

First off, felting wool is easy. All you need to felt wool is a washing machine! Your washing machine provides the three things needed for felting: agitation, heat, and moisture. Felting is basically a process that entwines or locks the fibers together, turning the fabric into a felt-like piece.

To felt wool, use a small amount of laundry detergent and the normal wash cycle, with hot water followed by a cold rinse. After washing, put the wool in the dryer on hot until it is completely dry. It's always best to keep like colors together, as dark colors may bleed during the felting process. This also ensures that you won't have dark lint fibers adhering to light fabrics, so you keep the wool looking nice. Be sure to clean the lint trap of your dryer often, as fibers build up quickly.

When you felt wool, it's hard to know how much it will shrink in the process, and the results may vary from one wool to another. Shrinkage will generally range from 10% to 20%. Differences can be due to settings used during the felting process, such as how hot the water is and how long the wool is agitated, for example. The more you felt wool, the better you'll be able to predict shrinkage. Always remember, for best results use 100% wool whenever possible.

Supplies for Wool Appliqué

The best part about working with wool is that you need very few supplies and no fancy gadgets! In fact, once you learn the technique and prepare the appliqués, all you need to finish your project will be scissors, thread, and a needle. How cool is that?

FUSIBLE WEB

Since my technique is based on using fusible web, you will not need the freezer paper, templates, or glue sticks that some methods require. All you need is a package of Soft Fuse Premium fusible web. Soft Fuse is the *only* product I use when creating wool projects.

Soft Fuse is a paper-backed fusible web for both machine and hand appliqué. The main reason I *love* working with it is that it does not gum up the needle. You can stitch through it with ease, making for a pleasant stitching process. It also makes your project portable once the pieces are fused in place. Soft Fuse comes in various sizes, starting with 8" × 9" sheets in a package of 10 for smaller projects and in widths starting at 18" for larger projects.

NEEDLES

When it comes to needles, I suggest chenille needles. I use chenille needles in two sizes, 20 and 22. These needles are designed with a long, large eye and a sharp tip, making them easy to work with when using floss in heavier weights. The long eye is less abrasive on the thread, and the sharp tip creates a hole in the wool that allows the thread to pass through easily. An added bonus is that these needles make threading your needle a breeze! With that being said, I strongly encourage you to use whatever needles you feel most comfortable using.

MARKING TOOLS

Pencils. I always have a package of mechanical pencils on hand. I like sharp pencils to trace the pattern shapes onto the fusible web. Mechanical pencils also eliminate the need to have a sharpener on hand. I like a nice crisp line, so I can easily see it when cutting out the shapes.

Marking pens. To mark on wool, a White Marking Pen (Fine) by Clover and a chalk pen are two of the items many of my students like using. These pens work great for drawing on dark fabrics or wool, and both pens are water soluble, making the marks easy to remove.

IRON

When choosing an iron, my only suggestion is to have an iron with steam. You'll need to use steam when fusing the appliqués.

THREADS AND FLOSS

These days, there's no end to the options for the type and weight of thread and floss to use. This is a good thing, but at times it may be overwhelming. To begin, I suggest using pearl cottons, six-strand embroidery floss, and wool thread. Within these three types, you'll have plenty of choices to enhance your projects. The more you stitch, the more you can learn and play with thread and floss. They can become another design element to enhance your projects.

Pearl cotton. I do 90% of my stitching with 12-weight pearl cotton, which is comparable to three strands of embroidery floss. I love this weight and find that I can use it on most any project. The best part is that it comes in both solids and hand-dyed colors. My preference, nine times out of ten, would be hand-dyed colors. I love how the shades flow on the wool.

Six-strand embroidery floss. I rarely complete a project without including a few of the standard, often-used colors of embroidery floss. I use two strands of floss for the smaller details, because using less floss helps to maintain the shape of little pieces. Like pearl cotton, there are both solid and hand-dyed options for embroidery floss.

Wool floss. Over the last couple of years, there has been a surge of wool floss on the market. Just like the two options of floss mentioned above, wool floss is available in different weights and colors. I'm just beginning to use more wool floss, and I'm pleased with the way it brings a new twist to my projects. Again, I would encourage you to use what you have and to experiment with new options that become available.

Wool Appliqué

Because the projects are made using the fusible appliqué method, all of the appliqué patterns are reversed. Follow these steps for fusible appliqué.

1 Place the fusible web, paper side up, over the pattern.

2 Trace each pattern piece separately. If one shape overlaps another, be sure to include the extra wool that goes underneath, as shown by dashed lines in the patterns. When tracing the pattern pieces, leave approximately ¼" of space between the traced shapes, and label each one. If you have pattern pieces that will be cut from the same piece of wool, trace them close together on the fusible web.

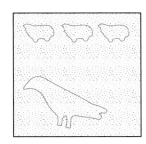

3 Roughly cut out each piece, leaving at least ⅛" around the traced lines. You can keep together as a unit all shapes that are to be cut from the same wool.

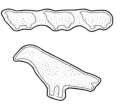

4 With the paper (traced) side up, lay the shapes close together on the chosen piece of wool but do not overlap them. Using your iron, fuse the paper pieces to the wool, following the manufacturer's instructions. While most wool is the same on both sides, take care to fuse the pieces to the side that you want to be the wrong side.

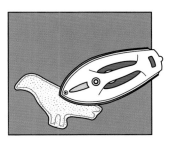

5 After the shapes have cooled, cut them out on the drawn line.

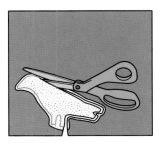

6 Referring to the pattern and the project photo, arrange the pieces on the background. When you have all of the pieces arranged, remove the paper backing from each wool piece and place the piece back in the layout. Be sure the pieces are layered correctly. Carefully press down on the pieces with a hot iron, using lots of steam to secure the appliqués in place. Press down for just a few seconds, and then gently move the iron around to fuse all the pieces in place. It's important to use a lot of steam, as the fusible web needs to melt between the wool pieces to secure them in place. You can always go over them again if there's a piece or two that did not fuse securely. When everything is fused, turn over the entire piece and steam it from the back.

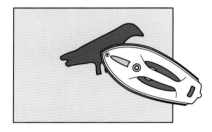

7 After the piece cools, stitch around the appliqués using the blanket stitch or whipstitch.

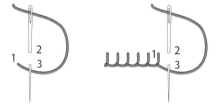

Blanket stitch

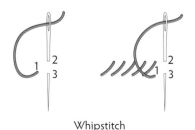

Whipstitch

Embroidery

When stitching the embroidered designs in this book or embellishing your wool projects, feel free to be creative and use the stitches you prefer in whatever colors and types of floss you prefer. That is the beauty of handwork! If you're unfamiliar with embroidery, refer to "Embroidery Stitches" on page 77 for a few basic stitches to try.

To transfer an embroidery design onto the background fabric, you can use a window or light box. A light box is easier, but a window works too.

1 Lay the pattern on the light box or tape it to a window.

2 Position the fabric over the pattern and trace the design lightly with a black or brown permanent fine-point marking pen. Be sure to use a fine-point marker so the lines will not show after you've stitched over them.

Embroidery Stitches

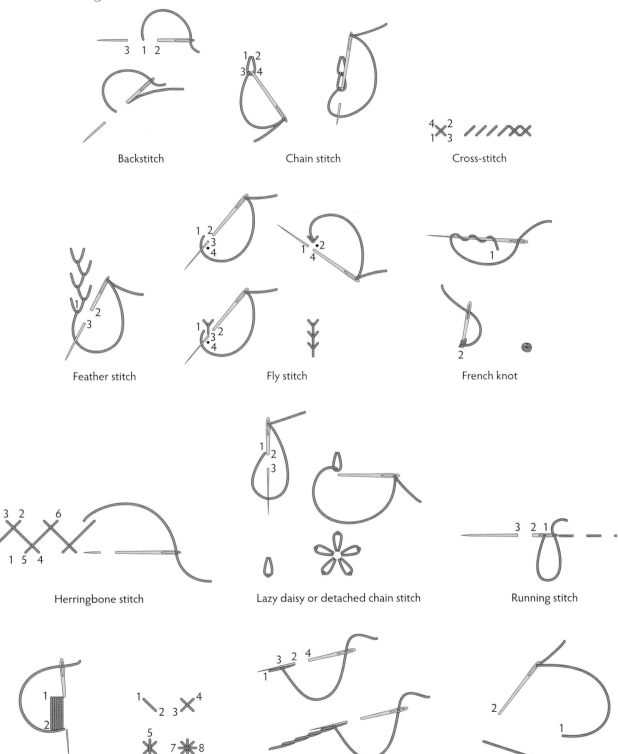

Backstitch

Chain stitch

Cross-stitch

Feather stitch

Fly stitch

French knot

Herringbone stitch

Lazy daisy or detached chain stitch

Running stitch

Satin stitch

Star stitch

Stem stitch

Straight stitch

Adding a Hanging Sleeve

1. Before sewing the binding on, measure across the top edge of the quilt. Cut a 6"-wide fabric strip 1" longer than the measurement.

2. Fold under ¾" on the short ends, toward the wrong side of the fabric. Stitch ½" from the fold to create a hem.

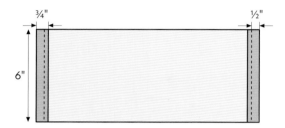

3. Fold under ¾" along one long edge of the strip and stitch ½" from the fold.

4. Place the strip on the back of the quilt, with the wrong side facing the quilt back and the raw edge along the top edge. Pin in place.

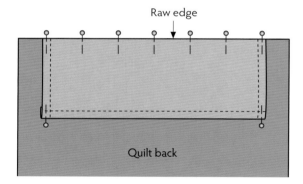

5. As you sew the binding on, you will sew the top of the sleeve to the quilt. Pin and stitch the bottom edge of the sleeve to the quilt by hand, being careful to stitch through the backing and batting only, not the front of the quilt.

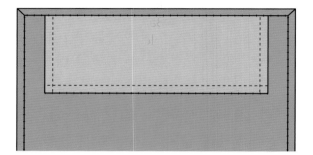

Acknowledgments

There are many special gals who have helped me with these projects; they've also been huge supporters of Buttermilk Basin and me. They have made this journey a blessed one. I'd like to introduce some of my *fave* peeps and share how their talents have been used within this book.

Jodi Daniels has been with me since back in the day, and she is now my shop manager. She started out rug hooking samples for me. She is also an avid sewist, unafraid to tackle any crazy project I come up with! She loves to put my quilts and block-of-the-month projects together for me. We have grown and learned *sew* much together. Each week we're working on something together here at the Basin.

Sheri Glasscock is a shop owner who shares with me a love for handwork and all things primitive. With her shop, she has supported my line of designs since day one. She puts her fun twists on my designs whenever she receives a new pattern. She, Kelly Hopkins, Carole Charles, and Pam Hansen have contributed their amazing talents in quilting the designs. Each one has a unique style that I have come to appreciate.

Kelly Hopkins started out doing punchneedle samples for me and now is one of my shop gals. She is a jill-of-all-trades. Usually she stitches wool projects and does my quilting. She has a stitching project in her hands on a weekly basis.

Kristina Tagarino is another talented and swell gal with whom I have enjoyed working. She contributed darling and creative stitches on the Crazy-Stitched Pineapple Mat in this book.

Karen Perry is a good friend who stitches for me. She also likes to put her creative twists on things after she receives a pattern, so sometimes I snatch one for a book project. Thanks, Karen!

Joey Cramer is another talented gal who works in almost any medium. Our paths first crossed at a local quilt shop. After I saw her redwork quilt, I knew I needed to have her as part of my team. She, too, stitches and sews and is a shop gal at Buttermilk Basin.

I also want to thank my husband, George. From the moment our paths crossed, you embraced my creativity and encouraged me to follow my dreams. I love you! To my daughters, Hannah and Grace, here is a quote from George Lucas: "Dreams are extremely important, you can't do it unless you imagine it." Always dream big. I love you both!

I'd like to thank my mother, Linda Gross, who, up until she passed away three years ago, was my main stitcher and biggest fan. She sewed dolls and stitchery for our previous company while I did wood crafts. Not a day goes by that I don't miss having her here creating with me.

To all the special people I've listed and to all my Buttermilk Basin supporters, a big thank-you! I appreciate all you do to help make my creative journey amazing. I would not be here if it weren't for all your help, love, and support along the way.

Resources

Buttermilk Basin Design Studio
8535 Central Avenue NE #102
Spring Lake Park, MN 55434
buttermilkbasin.com

Buttons, wool, yarn-dyed homespuns, cotton prints, patterns, and kits

About the Author

Stacy West is an artist who grew up in rural Minnesota surrounded by three generations of creative women. She learned to sew at an early age and studied graphic design in college. Stacy has never strayed far from fabrics and crafts as she worked at the local Ben Franklin in town, vended at numerous craft shows with her mother, and continued to work in a fabric store after college while designing for various craft magazines and continuing to sell her handcrafts.

In 1999, she and her mother, her partner in stitching nd crafting, displayed and sold their wares from a booth at International Quilt Market in Minneapolis, Minnesota. Stacy has been growing her business, Buttermilk Basin, featuring her original designs in wool and cottons. With products available online and at her thriving shop in Spring Lake Park, Minnesota, Buttermilk Basin is both a retail business selling wool, patterns, kits, fabrics, and home goods, as well as a wholesale supplier of her line of vintage-inspired patterns.

Stacy has become recognized as an innovator, nationally known teacher, and prolific designer in the quilting industry. She hosts three-day fiber retreats twice a year, and her work has appeared in a variety of magazines, including *Simply Vintage, American Patchwork & Quilting* and *Quilts and More.* She and her husband, George, have two daughters, Hannah and Grace, who love being a big part of Stacy's creative journey!